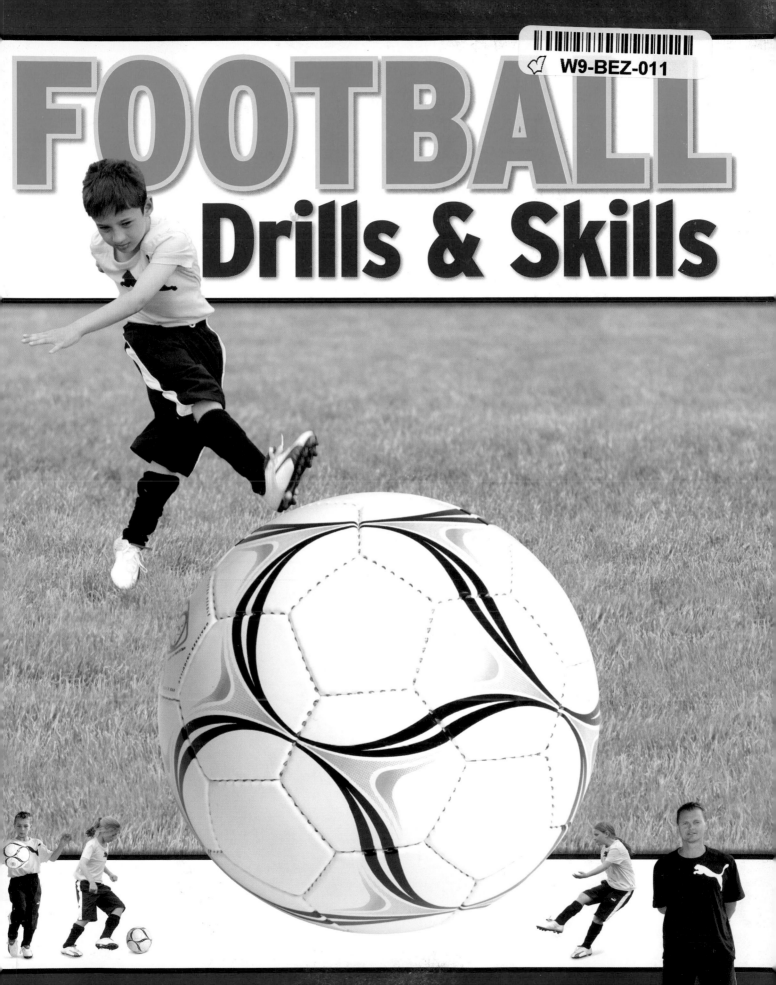

FOOTBALL
Drills & Skills

Michael Petersen

Creative Director: Sam Grimmer
Photography: Ned Meldrum and Darryl Snowdon
Prepress: Graphic Print Group

First published in 2006
by Hinkler Books Pty Ltd
17-23 Redwood Drive
Dingley Victoria 3172 Australia
www.hinklerbooks.com

© Hinkler Books Pty Ltd 2006

Thanks to:
Puma Australia
South Melbourne F.C.
Bayside Regional U13 Squad

Printed and manufactured in China

HINKLER
BOOKS

ISBN-10: 1 7415 7622 9
ISBN-13: 978 1 7415 7622 1

2 4 6 8 10 9 7 5 3
07 09 11 10 08

CONTENTS

INTRODUCTION

It's known as 'The World Game'. In some places they call it 'soccer', but to the vast majority, it's simply 'football'. Whatever name it goes by, one thing is for certain – it's the most popular sport in the world and its popularity is growing at a rapid rate.

Welcome to *Football Drills and Skills*, your personal coaching clinic. There are so many skills and drills here that they'll keep you practising and working hard!

Football Drills and Skills will help you to recognise the skills you need to play football well. It is packed with exercises and routines to help develop those skills, whether you are practising alone, with a partner, or in a group.

You'll also find out some background on the game, and a rundown on the rules and tactics.

Football is fast, skilful and at times, breathtaking. Its players are some of the biggest superstars in world sport.

Its fans are the most colourful and passionate, its stadiums the most famous sporting venues on the globe.

And every top football player started as a kid kicking a ball against a wall, around the yard or in a local park, with the dream of becoming a star.

Maybe that's why they call it 'The Beautiful Game'.

Michael Petersen

Former Australian Socceroo

THE GAME

Football was first played in England in the 1800s. Since then, it has grown to become the only sport played in every country on this planet.

The organisation in charge of football all over the world is called FIFA (Fédération International de Football Association). FIFA runs the World Cup, which is held every four years. It is the most-watched sports event on Earth!

The name football suits this sport very well, as you do not use your hands while playing (unless you are the goalkeeper).

In the game of football, two teams play against each other. A team is made up of 11 players, who play on a rectangular field, with goals at either end. There are set positions; a goalkeeper, defenders, midfielders and forwards (strikers). It is a sport where skill is the key, but speed, fitness and understanding of the game are also very important.

The Goalkeeper

plays a huge role in a football team. Stopping the opposition from scoring goals is as important as getting goals for your own team. Most good goalkeepers are tall and agile. They also need to be good communicators, as they organise the defenders in front of them. Goalkeepers are courageous, as they often need to jump for high balls, dive for low balls or throw themselves at an opponent's feet. Because a goalkeeper can use their hands, the skills they require are different from the other players on the team.

Italy's Dino Zoff, Denmark's Peter Schmeichel and France's Fabian Barthez (even though he is not tall!) are among the greatest goalkeepers ever.

Defenders

mainly try and stop the opposition from scoring. The best defenders are the ones who also start their team's attacking moves by making good passes for the midfielders and forwards. Defenders are usually strong players who are good tacklers, but have the speed to keep up with opposition forwards. Being a good header of the ball is also a big advantage.

Some of the best defenders of all time include Brazil's Roberto Carlos, Italy's Paolo Maldini and Germany's Franz Beckenbauer.

Midfielders

are the ones that keep a football team going. They do the most running during the game and are in action most of the time. This is because the ball moves through the midfield as teams attack and defend. The best midfielders are good at bringing the ball forward with their feet (known as dribbling) and make good passes to their team's forwards. But they also know how to defend when the opposition has the ball, and can win back the ball by tackling.

Midfield maestros of the world game include France's Zinedine Zidane and Patrick Viera, Brazilian Ronaldinho and David Beckham of England.

Forwards

(also called strikers) have a clear job in a game of football – they are there to score goals. And nothing in football is more thrilling than having your shot or header hit the back of the net. If they are not scoring, forwards are busy setting up scoring chances for their fellow strikers or midfielders. There are two types of players who make good strikers - the fast, skilful players who use their pace and ball control to get to the goals, or the stronger, taller types who have powerful shooting ability and are good at winning headers.

The two players regarded as the greatest of all time, Pelé from Brazil and Diego Maradona from Argentina, were both strikers, while modern legends like Brazil's Ronaldo, Holland's Ruud Van Nistelrooy and France's Thierry Henry are all goal-scoring machines.

SKILLS

Kicking is one of the first sporting skills we develop. At the park you might see kids as young as two years old kicking a ball across the grass.

Football Drills and Skills will help you take the most basic skills (like kicking) and improve them. It will also teach you to develop additional skills to make the game of football even more enjoyable.

Football skills revolve around kicking, as the foot is the part of the body that is most often in contact with the ball.

There are ways of kicking the ball to make delivery more accurate or powerful. There is a lot to learn about which part of the foot is used to kick the ball, where on the ball you make contact and what the rest of your body should be doing at the moment of impact.

Then you need to know about bringing the ball under control so that you can do what you want with it. You'll learn about running with the ball so it stays close to the feet and winning possession of the ball when an opposition player has it.

Of course you also need to know about using the other parts of the body, like the head, chest or thigh as another part of your footballing skills.

In many ways it's similar to learning the alphabet before you attempt to start making words and sentences. Like great writers or poets who have mastered language, when you master the skills of football you will also be able to create something magical.

So let's look at the ingredients that make a complete footballer.

> **Fastest goal**
> *Based on video evidence, Ricardo Olivera (Uruguay) scored in 2.8 seconds for Rio Negro against Soriano at the José Enrique Rodó Stadium, Soriano, Uruguay, on 26th December 1998.*

KICKING

Kicking is easy right?
We've been kicking since we were little kids, kicking our legs in the air, kicking at stones on the street, or balls of different shapes and sizes.

Many of today's top players didn't always have a football available to them when they were young so they came up with clever ways to practise kicking, from taped-up oranges to tennis balls. Volleyballs or netballs will do, as long as you find something round and soft enough to kick and have some fun!

To be a great kicker of a football, your technique has to be perfected to ensure that you are maximising your chances of making a successful pass, cross or shot on goal.

In this section of *Football Drills and Skills*, you will learn to go from the casual kick-about, to becoming a footballer that is passing, crossing and shooting with purpose and accuracy.

There is a lot more to a good kick than just your foot making contact with the ball. Your body posture and positioning is the key to getting the right result, and using different parts of your foot greatly impacts on the eventual delivery of the ball. Connecting with different sides of the ball will also impart speed and swerve on the football.

You probably like to use one foot more than the other, but to become a good player it's important to practise with both feet. You won't always find the ball is on the stronger side of your body, so being able to use your weaker side is a huge advantage.

Let's kick up a storm!

Female record for juggling (feet, legs and head)
Duration: 7hr 5min 25sec
Holder: Cáudia Martini (Brazil)
Place: Caxias do Sul, Brazil
Date: 12th July 1996

PASSING

There is a lot more to passing than just exchanging the ball between teammates. Passing glues together a team's play, it turns defence into attack, switches the direction of play and creates goal-scoring opportunities. You need to be able to pass the ball quickly and accurately even under pressure from the opposition.

SIDE FOOT PASS

You can use different parts of your foot to make a pass. The safest is the inside of the foot. It is the most basic and accurate form of passing as it means using the widest area of your foot. This cuts down the chances of making an inaccurate pass and it is ideal for short distances.

   You should be aware of your body position, with your weight shifting forward and your head over the ball.

• Get your body in line with the player you are passing to.

• Have your non-kicking foot beside the ball with the front toes of this foot pointing to where you want to pass it. Having your non-kicking foot close to the ball will ensure the ball is struck at full strength.

Never kick the ball with the point of your toes. Apart from being a very inaccurate way to kick the ball (because there is only a small, pointy bit that connects with the ball) it can also hurt!

OUTSIDE FOOT PASS

You won't always have the time to get into perfect position to make an accurate side-foot pass. Therefore players shouldn't limit themselves to one style of passing and should explore other techniques.

Passing with the outside of the foot is a quicker means of passing when the ball is to one side of your body.

But because there is a smaller area of your boot connecting with the ball, there is a greater chance the pass will not be accurate.

INSTEP PASS

The instep pass or 'drive' allows you to hit longer passes when you are either standing still or on the move.

• Your shoelaces should make contact with the middle of the ball and the follow-through should be long and smooth.

• Put your arms out for balance and plant your non-kicking foot right next to the ball.

• Swing your kicking foot back and then forward with your toes pointing to the ground.

• As you make contact with the ball make sure you connect with the outside of your foot.

CROSSING

Here is an interesting statistic to think about: over 60% of all goals come from wide positions that involve crossing the ball.

So you should pay special attention to the skill of crossing and understand the key points involved in making a good cross, which will hopefully give your strikers a chance to score your all-important goals.

Goalkeepers get very uncomfortable when a cross is delivered with the right amount of pace and curl. All that confusion leads to one thing: a great chance to score.

Defenders also find it hard to deal with good crosses because they are getting dragged out of position and are forced to make desperate lunges to protect the goal.

Players need to work together to get success. There is no point having sent in a fantastic cross and finding that there is no one to kick or head the ball home (if your teammates haven't realised what you were trying to do). So timing and synchronising with the rest of your team is crucial.

To make a perfect cross, you must know the right body positioning, the correct part of your foot to use and also the section of the ball that is struck to create the right amount of swerve.

So let's get going.

> **Largest football match attendance**
> *199,854 people attended the World Cup match Brazil v Uruguay in the Maracana Municiple Stadium, Rio de Janeiro, Brazil in July 1950.*

HIGH CROSS

More often than not, you will find a defender between you and your intended target. In this case a high cross is needed to get the ball past that first defender and into the danger area in front of goal. To achieve this:

- Lean back slightly on impact to lift the ball.

- The boot connects underneath the ball to make sure it goes up in the air.

- The part of the foot used is the upper instep (around where the big toe joins the foot), which will generate enough power to get the ball high and enough control to make the cross accurate.

Notice how the body is leaning back from centre. The point of contact with the ball is underneath. The follow-through shows the kicking leg swinging across the body.

- Look up and check where it would be best to cross the ball for your striker.

- Position your body in a more upright style than you would to deliver a high cross, with your head over the ball.

- Strike the middle section of the ball with a crisp, clean kick and good follow-through.

- Use your high instep, for power and accuracy.

LOW CROSS

At other times you will find yourself in a position to cross the ball without a defender in front of you or between you and your teammate. Maybe you have been able to dribble past the defence, or a teammate has given you a great pass that puts you out on your own. Here a low cross is in order and this type of delivery is easiest for your teammate to control and then shoot at the goal.

BENDING

When your team receives a free kick or a corner, the cross is hit when the ball is still, or 'dead'. This is a chance to impart swerve on the ball, to make it even more difficult for defenders to clear. To swerve, or 'bend' the ball:

- Lean back slightly on impact as you would to make a high cross.

- Strike the ball underneath, but to the outside of the ball to help put sidespin on it.

- Exaggerate the follow-through to maximise the sidespin you have placed on the ball.

SHOOTING

Now we're talking! The whole idea of the game is to shoot as many goals as possible to win. Connecting well with a shot and seeing the ball going in the goal is definitely one of the biggest thrills in football. That's why everyone, even the professionals, celebrate so much when a goal is scored.

But before you get to celebrate you have to score a goal, which is no easy task in a game of football. The goal is not very big and there is always a goalkeeper and a group of defenders trying to stop you. If you can develop a good shot, which requires both power and accuracy, you will be on your way to being a shooting star. So let's shoot to thrill!

INSTEP DRIVE

The instep drive is the shooting technique you will most frequently use. The key points to mastering this technique are:

- As you strike the ball, your knee is placed over the ball so as to ensure the ball is driven low. Also, your body posture should be slightly crouched and have forward momentum.

- The part of the foot you are using is the same as with the instep pass (see page 11). The full instep is in use.

- You should be looking to strike the ball right through the middle to generate power.

The way the ball bounces around the football field means that often it will not drop at your feet perfectly for you to apply the basic shooting technique. When the ball comes more awkwardly it can still be hit at goal, and often in a more spectacular way.

THE VOLLEY

The volley is made when the foot and the ball connect in mid-air. Because you can get the full force of your body into this kick it is one of the most powerful shots you can make.

SIDE VOLLEY

• Lean back a little from the oncoming ball.

• Swing your leg up and around.

• Make contact with your instep. Make sure your foot is over the ball to keep it down and follow through smoothly and firmly.

Always look to keep the ball low and on target. Always follow up your shot or a teammate's in case of rebounds. Don't be afraid to take a shot! The ball will not score a goal alone.

FRONT VOLLEY

• Lift your knee and point your toes down.

• Keep your head above your kicking knee.

• Look for a clean contact to send the ball in the direction you want.

BALL CONTROL

Who is your best friend in the whole world? Well, if you truly love the game of football then your answer is obvious: the ball! It is always there for you and you never get into arguments.

Great players from all over the world often say that while they were growing up, whether they were at school or at home with their families, even when they were away on summer holidays, the one thing that was by their side the whole time was a football.

And that brings us to the world of ball control.

Ball control is about being able to receive the ball in any situation and then manoeuvring both yourself and the ball into a position to complete the next move. That might be a long kick to relieve the pressure on your defence, a pass to a teammate or a shot at goal. If you have great ball control, other skills like dribbling and shooting will also improve.

The great players of world football have astonishing skills in manipulating a ball and making it look easy. It is almost like the ball is part of their body. Even the great Maradona practised with a golf ball!

But like everything, this skill does not come naturally and these players have spent many long, enjoyable hours with their best friend, the football.

Ball control is not just about working your left and right foot. You might receive a high-flying ball, which you will need to control on your thigh or even your chest.

We need to use every part of our body within the laws of the game (no hands) to gain control of the ball and give ourselves a better chance of making a great pass, dribble or shot on goal.

The best way to develop ball control on your own is by juggling. Unlike street performers and circus acts, football juggling is done by using all parts of the body apart from the hands (feet, thighs, chest and head) to keep the ball off the ground.

Gain control of yourself and let's get started.

> **Male record for juggling (feet, legs and head)**
> Duration: 19hr 30min
> Holder: Martinho Eduardo Orige (Brazil)
> Place: Ararangua, Brazil
> Date: 23rd August 2003

LOWER FOOT CONTROL

Just like your kicking technique, you can use all parts of your feet to bring a ball under control.

INSIDE FOOT CUSHIONING

- Get into position early with your weight on your supporting leg.

- Watch the ball until it contacts your foot on the inside.

- Bring your foot back slightly to bring the ball down.

INSTEP CUSHIONING

- Get your foot up with the instep facing the ball and your toe pointing slightly down.

- As the ball arrives bring your foot down with the ball resting just above it.

OUTSIDE FOOT CUSHIONING

- Get into position early with your weight on your supporting leg.

- Watch the ball until it contacts your foot on the outside.

- Bring your foot back slightly to bring the ball down.

UPPER CHEST CONTROL

CHEST CUSHIONING

• Take a wide stance for balance.

• Lean backwards as the ball reaches your chest – this will cushion the ball.

• As it drops down in front of you, get your foot on the ball as quickly as possible to gain control.

MIDDLE THIGH CONTROL

THIGH CUSHIONING

• The upper part of your leg should be almost parallel with the ground.

• Pull your leg down and back as the ball makes contact. This will slow down the ball's pace and should leave it in front of you.

DRIBBLING

Now here is a great crowd pleaser. Imagine, you've just controlled the ball beautifully and it is sitting nicely near your foot. You look up and there they are – three opponents wanting to take possession of the ball. No teammates are in position to take a pass, so off you go, down the field with the ball at your feet, outgunning the opposition with your speed and control of the ball. A few dribblers to watch are Brazil's Ronaldinho and England's Joe Cole. That's what we call dribbling!

To be able to run with the ball under control, turn, change direction and eventually deliver a good pass or a cracking shot at goal is one of football's most spectacular skills.

Dribbling is best done in the attacking half of the field, so you don't risk losing possession next to your own goal where the other team can take advantage and score. The aim of dribbling is to finish a move by doing something advantageous for your team, like a pass, a good cross or a shot. Merely running with the ball until you lose it gives the ball back to the opposition and puts your team back under pressure.

In this section we will look at dribbling in a straight line with speed. Then we'll look at changing direction while dribbling to avoid opponents. The great dribblers of football all have the ability to run with the ball and at the same time look up in case a teammate is in an excellent position to receive a pass. And it's a big part of football education – learning when to dribble and when to make a pass to a teammate who is in a better position.

Let's start with the basic techniques of dribbling.

Female player with the most national caps
270 by Kristine Lilly (USA) from 1987 to 2004.

DRIBBLING TECHNIQUE

While you are dribbling, you are mostly using the outside of either the left or right foot, as you are moving forward. You apply soft touches or flicks to the ball, whilst keeping it out in front of your body, no more than a metre or so, otherwise you are in danger of losing possession or control.

While ideally you will use the outside of your foot when dribbling, you may find there are occasions when you need to improvise to keep the ball under control. You can then use the instep of your foot to bring the ball back in line with your body.

CHANGING DIRECTION

You must be aware that in the course of a dribbling action other parts of the foot can come into play. If you want to change direction quickly, you can cut the ball with either the inside or outside of the foot.

- If you are running in a straight line and wanting to turn left, you can cut the ball using the inside of your right foot or the outside of your left foot.

- Similarly, to go from dribbling in a straight line to moving right, you can use the inside of your left foot or the outside of your right foot to push the ball right.

TACKLING

The ball will be in one of three situations in a game of football: either your team has it, the other team has it or it is in dispute.

When the other team has the ball it is your job to get it back and you do this by tackling.

Unlike other codes where tackling involves grabbing, dragging or pulling opponents to the ground, football is unique in that you can only use your legs to reclaim the ball. Timing must be precise, otherwise you will almost certainly give away a foul or free kick. Therefore you must win the ball cleanly and never kick an opponent, even by accident. So it is very important that when you attempt to tackle you must be watching the ball at all times.

On most occasions you will tackle an opponent who is running straight at you. To get the ball from them, you must execute a technique called the front block tackle, where you are face-to-face with your opponent with the ball between the two of you.

There will be other situations where your opponent has just slipped past, and the best you can possibly do is slide in from the side and get the ball with your legs before your opponent completely gets past you.

When an opponent is between you and the ball, you should not make a tackle. This is because you cannot reach the ball cleanly and will make contact with your opponent. For this, you will be given a foul.

Try to avoid fouls, because giving away too many free kicks will let your team down, particularly around the goal area. We've all seen David Beckham score wonderful free kicks from that vicinity.

Youngest hat-trick scorer in women's football
Amy Wilding (UK) was 15 years 200 days old when she scored 3 goals for Camberley Town Ladies against CTC Ladies in Croydon, Surrey, UK on 30th March 2003.

THE FRONT BLOCK TACKLE

The front block tackle is the most commonly used tackle, where you will usually be tackling an opponent from the front.

- Plant your non-tackling foot firmly on the ground.

- Lean forward into the tackle. This will give you a solid base.

- Use the inside of your foot to make strong firm contact with the middle of the ball. Often this will be enough to remove the ball from your opponent.

THE SLIDING TACKLE

Sometimes an opponent will get past with the ball. In this case your last chance is to employ a slide tackle, also known as a side tackle. Sometimes it's the only way to deflect or clear a ball.

- Make sure you bend your support leg at the knees.

- Slide in on your support leg as you make contact with the ball and transfer your body weight to your tackling leg and foot.

Tackling from behind is illegal. If an opposition player has their leg between you and the ball you can't possibly get the ball without kicking or fouling them.

HEADING

The ball is moving up and down continuously. Long kicks by the goalkeeper and long passes by players put the ball high up in the air. Sometimes you can't wait for the ball to drop and you do not have time to apply all the other skills you've learnt like passing and dribbling. You must go for the ball immediately and the rules allow for you to use your head to do so. There are many times in a game when you need to use your head.

Sometimes, you are under pressure from the opposition. Maybe a cross has been made and you have no choice but to clear the ball with a defensive header. You must be brave, otherwise your team could be in danger of conceding a goal.

Alternatively, one of your teammates might have kicked the ball into the penalty area and there is a great opportunity to score. You get there before the goalkeeper but you are forced to use your head, otherwise you will miss your chance.

This section will show you how to head the ball so it wont hurt you. Even a long kick out by the goalkeeper can be dealt with confidently because you connect with the correct part of your head. You need to know how to head front-on and how to head sideways, as the ball can come to you at different angles.

By bracing your neck muscles and having good body posture, heading is not only nothing to be afraid of, but can make you a valuable player for your team, particularly if you are one of the taller players. And it can be a lot of fun.

Let's get our heads around it.

Male record for juggling with head only
Duration: 8hr 12min 25sec
Holder: Goderdzi Makharadze (Georgia)
Place: Tbilisi, Georgia
Date: 26th May 1996

HEADING TECHNIQUE

Technique is very important when heading the ball. Remember to always use your forehead, never the top of your head. Don't be scared of the ball and try to keep your eyes open. Make sure your body is both balanced and relaxed. When jumping to head the ball you can use your arms for balance.

FRONT HEADER

• To put force into a front-on header, arch your back and thrust your upper body out.

• Keep your feet on the ground and head forward.

• Head through the ball, front-on, bracing your neck at the same time.

SIDE HEADER

As the ball may come from wide positions, the technique will be a flicking motion, depending which side the ball is coming from. Your header may be either a right-to-left or a left-to-right action.

GOALKEEPING

Because they are the only player on the field who can use their hands, goalkeepers are unique in a game of football. They even wear a different coloured uniform to the rest of the team. Common colours for 'keepers are all green or all yellow. They are also allowed to wear gloves so they can grip the ball better when they are making a save.

The goalkeeper is a team's final line of defence. You entrust your goalkeeper to do so many things. In fact, you may say they have the most amount of responsibility of all players on the field. Because the whole game is happening in front of them, they have the best view of what is going on. A goalkeeper needs to communicate with the defenders so they are organised in order to make it hard for the opposition forwards to get past them.

When the ball does get past the defence, the 'keeper is left with the task of saving their team. They can use their hands anywhere within the penalty area, but they can also use their legs and body to block shots at goal.

When the ball comes in high, the goalkeeper is expected to catch it, or to punch the ball to safety. When the ball is fired in low, the 'keeper should get their body behind it and smother it, or, if it is going wide, dive across and push the ball away to safety.

And if that isn't already enough, once they have control of the ball, safely in their arms, you then expect the 'keeper to distribute the ball correctly and get your team's possession moving. The 'keeper can do this by either throwing or kicking the ball.

Let's look closer at the tasks a 'keeper must perform.

GOALKEEPER TECHNIQUE

The key to being a great goalkeeper is to be very flexible and agile with razor-sharp reflexes.

If you are a 'keeper, always attempt to get your body behind the ball. Then there is no chance of the ball slipping through if you mishandle it.

DIVING

Sometimes you don't have enough time for positioning and you must fling your body into action.

• Move across from a basic stance.

• Launch yourself off one foot and get your hands behind the ball.

• Use your body and arms to prevent the ball from popping out as you land.

All goalkeepers should be aware at all times of what position they have taken up.

The correct angle in relation to the shot can greatly reduce the chance of a goal.

Many times the ball will pop up high into the penalty area, and the keeper must catch it.

CATCHING THE BALL

• Catch the ball with your hands in a 'W' position to prevent it from slipping through.

• Bring the ball safely to your chest.

PUNCHING THE BALL

• Sometimes catching the ball will not be possible and a punch or a deflection is necessary.

DISTRIBUTION

Goalkeepers are also responsible for distributing the ball once it is in their possession.

THE KICK

- The 'keeper can kick the ball out of their hands using an instep volley or a half volley. This is an ideal way to cover distance (by sending the ball further out).

THE THROW

There are three ways to throw the ball that can be very accurate over short distances.

THE UNDERHAND ROLL OUT

- Point the front foot at the target.
- Release the ball and follow through smoothly.

THE JAVELIN THROW

- Bend the arm.
- Thrust it forward. This is often the quickest way of distributing the ball.

THE OVERHAND THROW

- Keep the arm straight.
- Swing over with a bowling motion.

TRAINING ON THE FIELD

You have just seen how many exciting skills are involved in the game of football. In your mind you can picture yourself delivering great passes, making a flying header, or waltzing by two defenders and scoring a goal. You can daydream for hours about all the wonderful things you will do on the football field.

To make it a reality you need to get your own body doing all the skills and manoeuvres.

The body is not like a television or computer where you can turn a switch on or off - you need to take much more care of it and prepare yourself correctly for the training sessions ahead.

There are football players over 50 years old still enjoying the game. The way to stay fit and healthy is by always warming up your body before practice and games.

Sometimes you may find it a little boring to do your stretches and warm up preparation but you can avoid soreness, stiffness and injury if you take your preparation seriously.

Remember, in amongst all the dynamic skills, thrills and spills of football, it is essentially a running game. Football players go up and down the field continuously; sometimes sprinting, sometimes jogging but moving all the time.

It is important for the game of football that you do various kinds of running exercises to improve and maintain fitness. You must work on your strength so that your sprint times can improve and also your stamina levels, so you can have energy for the whole game.

PREPARATION

Eating correctly will give you the right amount of fuel to perform at training and getting a good night's sleep will help you concentrate during the game.

Hydration is a very important word in sport. It refers to the amount of water we have in our body. Having enough fluid, or liquid, before and during a game or training is important so you don't get dehydrated.

Drink plenty of liquids – sports drinks or just plain water – before you do any physical activity and keep topping up through a game or a training session. It's a great idea to have your own water bottle, not just for health reasons, but because you can then keep track of just how much fluid you are taking in and make sure you are getting enough.

WARM-UP AND STRETCHES

Whether you are training or playing a game, it is important to run through a series of stretches and warm-up runs. Stretches include all the major leg muscles including the calf, hamstring, quad and groin.

Then you must stretch the neck and back muscles.

For a warm-up run, start with light jogging and slowly build up the tempo. Two or three laps of the field will be enough. After approximately 10 minutes you should be able to do a series of sprints that will prepare you for action.

If you do five 20 metre and five 10 metre sprints, this will be sufficient.

Finish with some last minute stretching.

You are now ready to play.

RUNNING AND FITNESS

Because running and fitness are a major part of football, you need to do running drills as part of your football training.

Your capacity to improve is boundless so don't be afraid to push yourself.

SPEED AND STRENGTH
Line up six cones five metres apart.

- Get ready at cone one.
- Sprint to cone two and return back to cone one.
- Go to cone three and return back to cone one. Keep going until you hit cone six, then return to cone one.
- Do five repetitions with a five-minute break in between.

> Do this drill at the end of your skill session to become fitter and stronger. Start timing yourself to see the improvement. When turning get down low, touch the ground or cone and push off. This drill will help you with stamina.

SPRINT

1   2   3   4   5   6

CHALLENGE
Create a rectangle like a football ground using six cones. Remember, the bigger the area the harder the exercise.

- Start at cone one, jog one lap clockwise.
- When you get back to cone one, sprint to cone two (as shown).
- Don't stop, but continue jogging around the rectangle.

- When you get back to cone one, sprint to cone three then start jogging back to cone one again to recover.
- Once you are back to cone one, sprint to cone four and jog back.
- Keep going until you sprint the full rectangle.
- Finish with one lap of jogging very slowly.

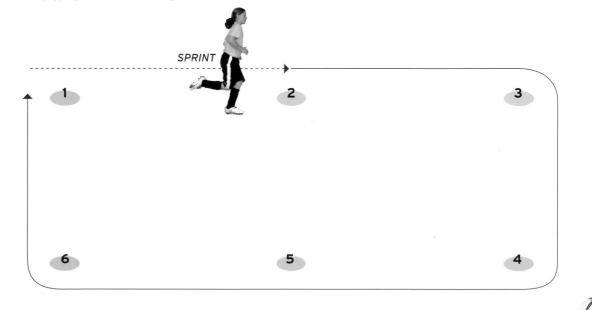

SPRINT

1   2   3

6   5   4

DRILLS

Now that you've looked at all the skills required to be a footballer, you need to take that knowledge out to the park or training ground and practise. The stars of the game didn't get there by talent alone. They put in hard work and dedication, and were determined to improve and be the best they could be.

The drills that follow are simple, but are ones that every footballer has done over and again to hone their skills. You can practise alone, with a friend or in a group. The aim is to make the ball an extension of your body, so you feel comfortable receiving, controlling and disposing of it. It should feel natural, something you could do with your eyes closed.

Never underestimate the value of repetition. If you have ever seen a player keeping the ball in the air with their feet, thighs and head it is because of the many hours they have spent practising. It is the same with passing, shooting, controlling and dribbling the ball.

The value in the following drills is in doing them often and challenging yourself by making them faster and more demanding.

PASSING DRILLS

SOLO PASSING

This drill is perfect if you are on your own and feel like practising your passing. If you have access to a solid wall with a smooth surface, you can practise all the techniques found in *Football Drills and Skills.*

• Start kicking from about 5 metres away, then progress to 10 metres and even 15 metres once you are feeling confident.

The ball will keep coming back to you very quickly. Remember to use the inside of your foot, the outside of your foot and the instep drive.

5–15 metres

PASSING DRILLS (CONT)

GROUP ON THE MOVE

Both players can practise their passing, however one player acts as a server.

- Stand 10 or 15 metres apart. (Feel free to change distances.)
- The player serving the ball knocks the ball 5 metres to the left of centre.
- The player working must react and control the ball and knock it back to the server, then return back to the centre.
- The server then passes it approximately 5 metres to the right of centre.
- Once again the player working must react and move to the pass and attempt to get the ball back to the server smoothly and quickly.
- Do 5 to 10 on the left and right sides then rotate the server.

Balance is important.

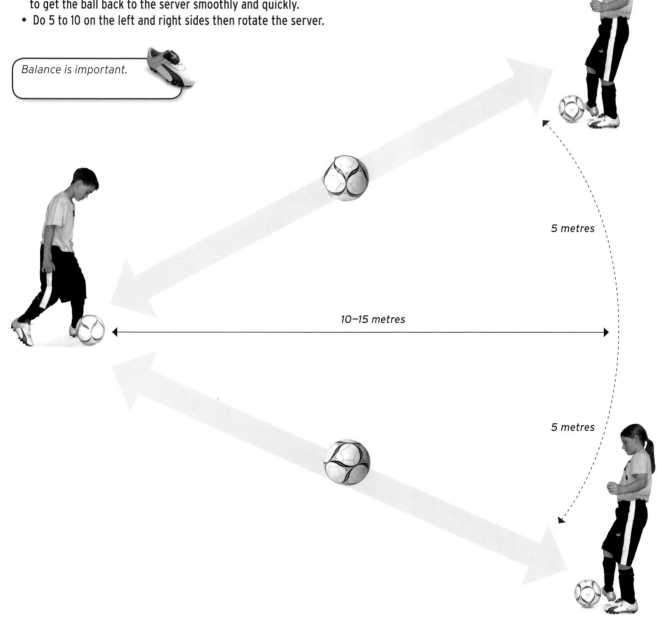

5 metres

10–15 metres

5 metres

DUO ON THE MOVE
- Stand 10 or 15 metres apart facing the halfway line.
- When you are ready, exchange passes while you work your way to the halfway line, then work your way back.

Timing, accuracy and weight of the pass are important. It may take some time to get fluent at this drill, but keep persisting.
Our aim is to ultimately take one touch to control the pass and one touch to make the pass.

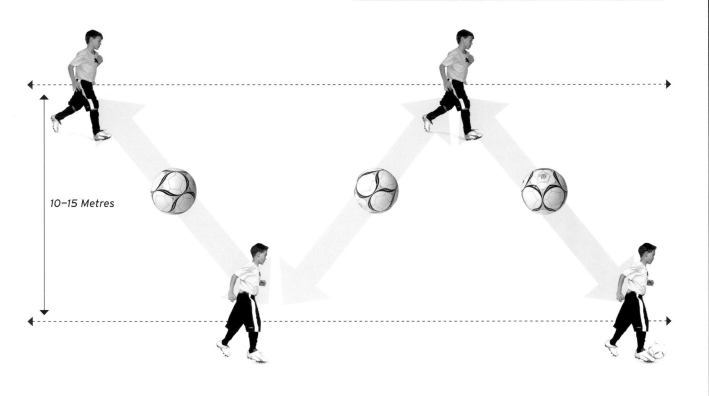

10–15 Metres

DUO PASSING
- Players stand 10, 15 or 20 metres apart.
- Each player marks out a square 5 metres by 5 metres with cones.
- The aim of the drill is to land the ball on the full in the 5-metre box area where your teammate is. If you are successful, give yourself a point. Take it in turns until one player reaches 20 points.

Remember you must hit the player on the full. Straight drives and side foot passes work well.

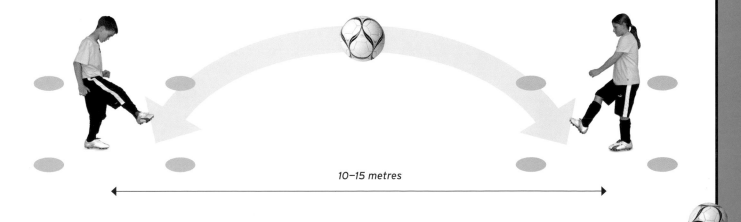

10–15 metres

SHOOTING DRILLS

SOLO SHOOTING DRILL

Go back to your brick wall. If it is possible (and you are allowed to), make some markings on the wall with chalk. If you can't, make your own mental zones.

- Make up your own game and see how many points you can get through hitting the different targets on the wall.
- Remember your shooting techniques and spend 15 to 20 minutes a day doing these exercises. You will be surprised how quickly you improve. It's a great feeling when you hit the target with a power shot!

- *Use your left and right foot, as you need to be good at both sides, even if one is stronger.*
- *Try some David Beckham curlers to hit the target.*
- *Pretend you are taking a corner and the target is your teammate's head or foot.*
- *Start kicking from about 5 metres away, then progress to 10 metres and even 15 metres once you are feeling confident.*
- *Enjoy yourself and don't be scared to make mistakes. Mistakes help you to improve and get better.*

5–15 metres

GOAL DRILL

You don't even need a goalkeeper to do this, but it's good to rotate the position if there are enough players. A number of balls are needed for this one. Using four to six balls is the best.

- Line the balls up in front of the goal and put a marker 10 metres behind you.
- Start 10 metres out (you can move further out as you get better at the drill).
- Strike a shot at goal.
- Run around the marker and shoot again.
- Continue until you run out of balls.

Kick half with your left foot and half with your right. Count how many goals you score.

| 10 metres | 10 metres |

GROUP SHOOTING DRILL

It's time to test your volley skills. Find any goal with a net. (It could even be a hockey goal, lacrosse goal or small football goal but preferably, a normal-sized football goal.)

- A player stands behind the goal with the balls and acts as a server.
- The player working stands 3 to 5 metres out from goal (as you get more confident, move further out).
- The server throws the ball underarm over the top of the goal.
- The player working attempts to connect with a volley and score into the net.

ADVANCED DRILL

So you have got your eye-foot coordination working well. Attempt the same drill but start downsizing balls. Try a size three ball, then size one ball. Then have a go with a tennis ball. If you master this drill, you will be scoring plenty of goals.

Have a minimum of five shots at goal then rotate the server.

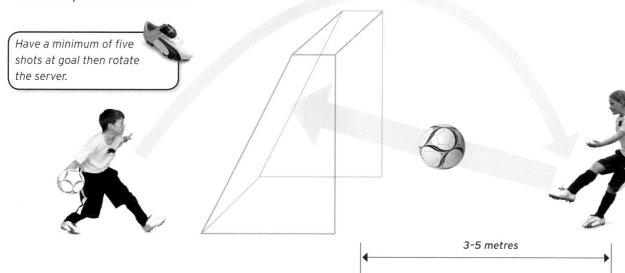

3-5 metres

BALL CONTROL DRILLS

SOLO BALL CONTROL DRILL

You can practise juggling almost anywhere and anytime. You just need a tiny bit of space and away you go. Really great players have the ability to juggle the ball and look like they could be in a circus! Brazil's Ronaldo is a great juggler.

• Start juggling the football, keeping it off the ground. Count how many times you touch it before it hits the ground: 4...8...12 and you are going well; 18...23...40 is very good; 60 is excellent and 100 – Ronaldo!
• Use both feet, your thigh, chest or head – whatever it takes to stop the ball from hitting the ground.

Remember – no hands. Be patient and don't put too much pressure on yourself. The most important thing is that you are enjoying yourself.

WALL DRILL

Again, our friend the wall is here to help us with this drill!

- Try bouncing the ball off the wall and control it without it hitting the ground.
- Count how many touches between you and the wall there are before the ball hits the ground.

This is a great way to learn how to receive the ball and it improves balance quickly.
If there are more players, you can pass the ball to each other.

ADVANCED DRILL

The stuff of superstars! If you do the above drills with a tennis ball, all the big football clubs around the world will sign you up, guaranteed! Zinedine Zidane and Thierry Henry are particularly good at controlling the ball.

BALL CONTROL DRILLS (CONT)

GROUP CONTROL DRILL

- Once you have some players, you can gather in a tight circle and share the ball around.
- Pass the ball without it touching the ground. Have as many touches as you like to begin with before passing it over.
- If someone makes a mistake, they must sit out until there is only one player standing. Equally, if you make a bad pass to another player, you must also sit out.
- As you and the group improve, reduce the number of touches allowed before passing. Ultimately your goal should be to have one-touch passes.

Enjoy the challenge of keeping the ball off the ground and all the time your football skills will be improving.

ADVANCED DRILL

As you master this drill, you can make it harder by using a size 3 ball or even a tennis ball.

DUO CONTROL DRILL

All you need is a partner and a ball for this one.

• Stand 2 to 3 metres apart with one of you holding the ball, acting as a
  server and the other acting as a receiver.
• Start with the lower body. The ball is served to the foot area of the receiver.
• The receiver returns the ball back into the arms of the server.
• Do 10 on the left foot and 10 on the right.

• Now you can progress to the middle body. The ball is served to the
  thigh area of the receiver.
• The receiver controls the ball on their thigh and passes it back to
  the server with their foot.
• Do 10 on the left and 10 on the right.

• Move onto the upper body. The ball is served to the chest area.
• The receiver cushions it and once again returns it by foot.
• Do 10–20 repetitions of this.

ADVANCED DRILL

*OK, hot shots! If you have
gone well so far, let's step
up a gear. The server
pitches to the chest area of
the receiver. The receiver
cushions the ball with their
chest and then lets it fall to
their thigh, where they again
cushion the ball. They then
let it fall to their feet and
return it to the server. That's
three actions all in one
motion! Good luck!*

2–3 metres

DRIBBLING DRILLS

SOLO DRIBBLING DRILL

You need to start with the most basic drill and then slowly progress.

- Place two cones about 10 metres apart (or further).
- Start at one cone and comfortably run with the ball toward the other cone, gently tapping the ball with either foot.
- Go around the marker and head back.

> When you are comfortable with this drill, time yourself to see your improvement. The quicker you go, the harder it is for opponents to stop you.

10 metres

HARDER DRIBBLING DRILL

As you get better, you need to keep challenging yourself and go to a higher level.

- Place 10 cones, 1.5 metres apart in a straight line.
- Dribble in and out of the cones, without hitting them.
- Go around the last cone and do the same on the way back.
- As you master this drill, you can make it harder by reducing the space between the cones to 1 metre.

> Time yourself to record your improvement. Remember to use both feet to negotiate your way through the cones.
> Watch Portugal's Cristiano Ronaldo and Australia's Harry Kewell, as they are experts in this area.

1.5 metres

ADVANCED DRILL

Now your balance and touch control will be tested. You will be zig zagging and moving diagonally all in the same motion. Good luck! Again we use 10 cones or markers that are 1.5 metres apart. Go round the first cone then cut the ball back to make it round the next cone. Keep going and do the same on your way back. Now cut the ball with the inside of your foot then change back to the outside of your foot.

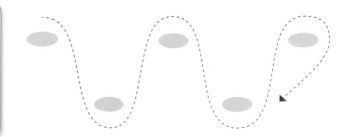

TACKLING DRILLS

SOLO TACKLING DRILL

The best way to practise tackling is to play small games, with either two, three or four players on each side. Tackling situations will come up all the time. However, you can also practise tackling by yourself.

- Place the ball against a wall and stand a few steps away from it.
- Plant your non-tackling foot firmly on the ground.
- Use the inside of your other foot to make a firm contact with the middle of the ball. This will give you a feel of what it is like to perform a block tackle.

DUO TACKLING DRILL

You can also set up a drill with two players.

- Put a ball in between you and stand a few steps apart.
- Both players tackle with the same foot (both tackle with the left foot, or both go with the right foot).
- On the count of three, both players step in with medium force to connect with the ball at the same time.
- Do 10 to 20 of these.

Make sure your timing is correct. Only apply medium force so no one gets injured. Alessandro Nesta of Italy is a particularly good tackler.

HEADING DRILLS

SOLO HEADING DRILL

For this drill, you just need yourself, a ball and a wall.

- Stand 2 to 3 metres from the wall.
- Serve the ball underarm against the wall so that it rebounds back towards you.
- Move your body and thrust your neck towards the ball.
- The aim is to head back to the wall.
- Catch the ball in your arms and serve again.

ADVANCED DRILL

As you get better, you won't need to use your arms at all. Just continue using the wall and your head. Count how many times you can do it in a row. 10 to 20 is great, 20 to 40, excellent! And anything over 50, you might need to call up the coach of Real Madrid!

If there are more of you, you can form a tight circle and head the ball around, keeping it off the ground. Achieving 50 headers in a group is outstanding.

3 metres

DUO HEADING DRILL

If you want to master jumping and heading at the same time, you need to work with a partner.

- Stand about 5 metres apart. One person will be server, one receiver.
- The server throws the ball forward in the air.
- At the same time, the receiver moves forward and jumps. The receiver should connect with the ball in mid-air and send it safely back.
- The server catches the ball and serves again. Do 10 to 20 then swap over.

> *Watch England's John Terry. He attacks the ball with his eyes open and scores heaps of goals!*

ADVANCED DRILL

This is where it gets tricky – when you have to challenge to win a header. You need a server and two players. The server stands around 5 to 10 metres away while the two combatants stand next to each other. The ball is then thrown up and forward in the air and the race is on to see who of the two players can win the header.

> *This drill will test your anticipation, timing, strength and aerial ability. Good luck and may the best header win! Remember to keep your elbows in when you jump to avoid injury.*

5 metres

PLAYING THE GAME

Practice definitely makes perfect, and while it's a great achievement to improve by training hard, nothing beats the excitement of actually being part of a team and playing in a match.

Your individual skills are designed to make you a better contributor to the team. It is important to be a team player on the field. Pass the ball to teammates and play in the position the coach has put you in.

Football is not about 11 players on a team chasing after the ball at the same time, trying to dribble the ball down the field on their own and score a goal. Defending, tackling and passing are all just as important as scoring.

You will be just as valuable to the team and should feel just as much pride if you do a good defensive job or pass the ball to someone to score a goal.

If your team scores, get in with everyone and celebrate, because that's the best part!

MATCH DAY

M atch day is always exciting. Make sure you have all your gear, like shorts, socks and shin guards, and make sure your boots are clean. Before playing a game of football, there are a few extra ingredients worth understanding to make it more enjoyable.

THE REFEREE

In addition to the 22 players (11 on each team) that take to the field in a game of football, there is also a referee who controls the game. The 'ref' will know the rules of football and will use their whistle to signal if anyone breaks them. The referee's job is to stop the game when they see things like tripping or handball.

The ref will also use the whistle to signal the start and end of the game, the ball going out of play and a goal.

The blowing of the whistle will usually be followed by an explanation of the decision.

Remember the referee is there to help your enjoyment of the game and their decision is final. Never argue with the ref or dispute their decisions, as this is bad sportsmanship and will not help you.

THE COACH

The coach, or manager, is in charge of running the team. The coach takes responsibility for training, selecting the team and deciding the playing tactics.

Basically, they are the boss and a good coach will be an excellent teacher, as well as someone who is admired. There is a saying that the best teams 'play for their coach'. What that means is that they are inspired to try their best and play their hardest for their leader.

SUBSTITUTES

In addition to the 11 players on the field, there are also substitutes who can come on and take another player's place at any time during a game.

Substitutes play an important role as they often come on when someone has been injured, runs out of steam or is simply not playing well. The coach may make a substitution for a tactical reason, or just to give everyone in the squad a run.

Some top players made their names as substitutes, or 'impact' players. They had a history of coming into the game and changing its course, earning the nickname 'super-sub'.

Ole Gunnar Solskjaer has gained a reputation as a super-sub and is known for often changing the course of a game (a famous game he 'won' for his team was the 1999 Champion's League final for Manchester United).

OFFSIDE

Offside is the rule that confuses most non-football followers, but is really quite simple.

When the ball is passed, kicked or headed forward, the player receiving the ball cannot be behind the last defender. That is, they cannot be between the opposition's goalkeeper and the defender closest to the goalkeeper. If so, they are receiving the ball in an offside position and a free kick is paid to the defending team.

Offside is judged from the time the ball is actually played through to the attacking player. As long as that player is even with or in front of the last defender when their teammate delivers the ball, they will be onside and able to keep playing.

A player can never be offside if they dribble past the defence on their own, or if a pass is played back to them from a more forward position.

The offside rule is designed to stop players from camping behind the defence and waiting for a long pass over the top. It therefore discourages teams from just booting the ball long into their forward line and puts the emphasis back onto the skills of controlling and passing the ball, and intelligent running to position to receive the ball.

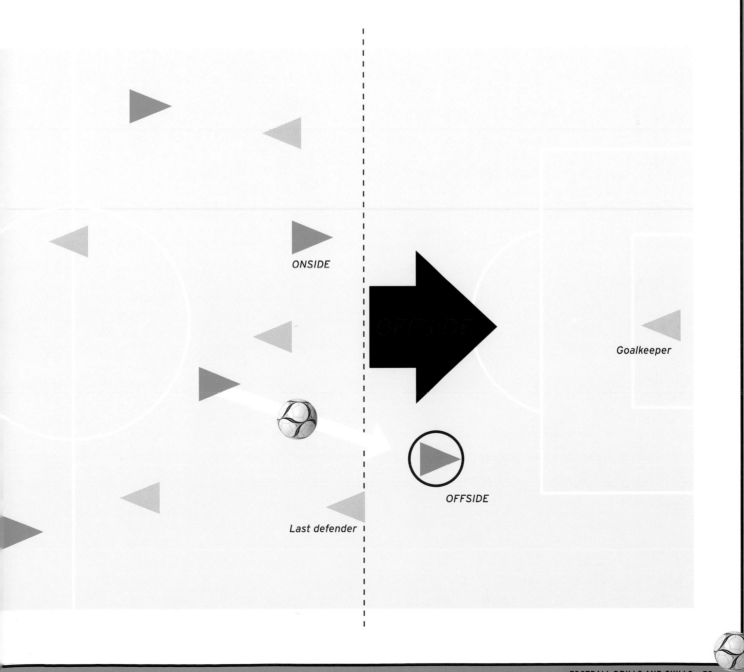

ONSIDE

OFFSIDE

Goalkeeper

OFFSIDE

Last defender

THROW-INS

When the ball goes out of play over the sideline, the referee will award a throw-in against the team that last touched the ball before it went out. This is the only time an outfield player uses their hands.

The ball must then be thrown in by one of the opposition team from where it went out of play and in a manner that conforms to the rules of football. There are three parts to this rule:

- The player's feet must be behind the sideline when they throw the ball back in.

- The ball must be held with two hands, be taken back behind the player's head and released with a throwing motion (not dropped).

- The player must have both feet on the ground when the throw-in is released.

If you take the throw-in in an incorrect manner or from the wrong place, the referee will blow their whistle and give the throw-in to the opposition.

CONCLUSION

Well, hopefully, you now understand what it takes to be a star on the football field!

There are many skills to master, and the importance of practice, practice, practice cannot be stressed enough.

Strength, speed and fitness are also all important ingredients that make up a good football player, so don't forget to work on these aspects, as well as your skill with the ball.

But one of the most important things is to be a good team player. Football is a team game and success comes when everyone does their job — from the goalkeeper through to the defenders, midfielders and strikers. And this includes substitutes, who need to come on and fit into the team structure when they get their chance on the field.

Always support your teammates. If someone makes a mistake (and we all do), don't get angry — encourage them to do better at the next opportunity. And involve your teammates in the game by passing the ball to them when they are in a good position and congratulating them when they do well.

It feels good to do something well as an individual, but it feels great to be part of a winning team.

Enjoy your football.

ABOUT THE AUTHOR

Michael Petersen progressed from local football with Port Melbourne juniors all the way to representing one of the most famous clubs in Europe, the mighty Ajax Amsterdam of Holland. In between he was a star midfielder in the Australian National Soccer League, first with Heidelberg United, before winning NSL championships with Brunswick and South Melbourne.

Returning to South Melbourne from Europe, Micky P, as he was known, became one of the club's favourite sons, finishing his playing career with South Melbourne before going on to coach the club.

Michael was selected to play for Australia against touring Italian club Udinese and made his A International debut against Taiwan in Canberra. He was a team member during three World Cup campaigns and part of the Australian Olympic team that reached the quarter-final stage at the Seoul Olympics. He played 51 matches for the Socceroos, including 32 A internationals and scored four goals.

He is now passing on his vast knowledge to the next generation of Australian Socceroos as assistant coach for the country's under 20s international team, known as the Young Socceroos.

Michael was recently inducted into Australia's Football Hall of Fame.